PREPPING AND SURVIVAL FOR NEWBIES

How to Survive in a Crisis or Disaster

By
Ernest Rivera

Disclaimer

The information contained in this book is for the purpose of general information and awareness. It is not intended as a one-size-fits-all advice for the prepping and survival interest. When in doubt, always make sure to consult an expert or professional in the relevant field. The author shall not be held liable for any loss or damage arising from any action or omission related to information contained in this book.

Table of Contents

Introduction

"War is not for winning, Masha," sighed Koschei,
reading the tracks of supply lines, of pincer strategies,
over her shoulder. "It is for surviving."
- Catherynne M. Valente, Deathless

Survival happens in our everyday life; everyone is trying to survive biologically; we do this by adapting and making a few changes to fit in just fine into our environment. There is no survival without these changes, which range from learning, re-learning, and making adaptive changes that put us on top of our games. Prepping is that change that reconfigures you better for survival irrespective of the odds, it is that closet where we are rebranded and packaged.

Prepping exceeds some doomsday anticipation; it is preparing yourself for the ultimate unlikely events. However, everyday preppers become better equipped to tackle various emergencies in society. They have gone from being dependent on the government to become guardians of their family in the occurrence of an unlikely event.

Since prepping can be really broad in scope, newbies are advised to start prepping by first identifying their fears. The only exception to this method of starting prepping is if you have plenty of money to spare when caught off-guard by an emergency.
Despite the multi-faceted nature of prepping, the prepping community provides a connection that allows for sharing some membership advantages. You could learn from another prepper who is preparing for an entirely different kind of unlikely event; in the occurrence

of unlikely events, the community of preppers would be invaluable.

It is important you note that irrespective of the sort of preparation you sign up for, in the occurrence of an unpalatable event, you are better equipped than folks who have not done any prepping. The silver lining in emergencies is the fact that all emergencies share some common ground. So, you may not be knowledgeable about dealing with specific events, but basic prepping would still give you an edge in such situations.

If you were to ask the governments, the odds are that they would encourage citizens to prep. People obviously only have issues with prepping because they are making financial commitments for an event that is unlikely to happen. But they do not realize that even presidents and heads of states have evacuation protocols for unlikely events. Everyone is prepping one way or the other!

I have tried to make this guide succinct and brief for newbies; if this is your first time learning about prepping and survival, try to read it once through understanding the main concepts. I recommend reading it at least twice, so that you could explore each section in greater detail.

This chapter is focused on defining the words that make up the prepping and survival field.

What is Prepping?

The Oxford dictionary defines prepping as the act of preparing for something; it further describes it as the practice of making active preparations for a possible catastrophic disaster or emergency, typically by stockpiling food, ammunition, and other supplies.

Simply put, prepping is the preparation you put in place for a wide range of emergencies.

Prepping has evolved to be more than a practice for some people; it has become a lifestyle; these folks are constantly living a life that can run successfully outside the make of our modern society.

This is evident by simple practices such as growing their personal food garden, buying safety gear for different emergencies, and more. Preparation for survival or extreme emergencies would require you to be ready for:

- A deficit in the food supply
- Lack of protective tools
- Inaccessibility of transport & communication channels
- Shutdown of electricity
- Other forms of emergencies. In early 2020, the COVID-19 viral pandemic was a major scare to most people. Some claim that the prepping

industry wasn't prepared for this Novel Coronavirus outbreak.

I am of the opinion that the skill set and training the prepping industry have equipped preppers with is highly relevant to tackling such pandemics. Since emergencies share some common attributes, there is nothing to lose by being prepared for a disaster.

Given that emergencies vary in the degree of severity and what effect they pose to humanity, there has to be levels of preparation. Levels of prepping (preparedness) are sometimes gauged by the period of distress and the intensity or effect on society. Based on these factors, prepping levels range from basic preparedness for short periods to preparing for emergencies that extend up to a year.

Levels of Prepping

- Basic preparedness is the first of four levels of prepping. It refers to a simple preparation for mild and short emergencies.

For example, most organizations would have a first aid kit in case of small cuts and injuries during work; other individuals have alternate plans in case of a blackout in their area. These preparations are made in case of mild emergencies, which are usually short-lived; there is nothing special about them, although the threat they pose would depend on the current situation.

The other three levels of prepping are not specifically named but are identified by the period of emergency.

- The second level of prepping covers emergencies/ disasters that would have an effect for up to 30 days
- The third level covers a period of three months or more
- The fourth level covers catastrophic events that would affect you for almost a year

With each level comes some necessities and intense preparation. A disaster that affects communication networks would require you to find some other means of communication; you would also require defensive equipment against hostile neighbors looking for supplies.

Irrespective of the nature and period of the disaster, prepping must be centered on some necessities. I would like to call them the pillars of prepping; they are the essential things prepping must cover.

Pillars of Prepping

If these pillars are absent in any preparation for emergencies, they do not meet the basic goals of prepping.

- **The art of accessing supplies**
  One of the fundamentals of prepping is teaching you how to access or acquire necessary supplies. Supplies range from food items to shelter, and every other item required for sustenance during the period of emergency. Preppers usually live their life prepared for these occurrences; some of them grow their own food, or always buy in bulk for reserve.

Aside from having supplies in reserve for food and cash, a prepper usually has the equipment for various kinds of emergencies. These supplies could range for communication channels, to alternate methods of sustaining and protecting themselves. In a later section, I will dive into the subject of necessary supplies, and include a checklist of items preppers must have.

- **The art of skills acquisition**
Preppers do not just have supplies to suffice them through and during disasters. Preppers have fine skillsets for survival. For example, a first aid kit is not of much use if you do not acquire the skills and knowledge to administer first aid correctly. Preppers learn a lot of skills for survival, ranging from self-defense, communication, and any skill specific to the disaster.
Supplies would sustain life and provide you with the necessary tools, but skills are the next determinant of your survival. For instance, in the event of a flood, being able to swim and hold your breath under water may give you a good chance of survival.

- **The Art of Building a Community**
Building a community is indispensable in prepping. Clearly, we humans are not know-it-alls. There is surely a need to connect with like-minded folks. In the occurrence of a disaster, we would have aid and assistance from these people. By complementing one another, it would be easier to survive and prepare for crises.
In addition, people would feel more secure and optimistic about survival when they are in groups

rather than on their own. Having a community of preppers also allows you to pool together your resources.

Why Prepping

Why prepping? When emergencies occur, it becomes a test of who is most prepared and able to overcome the challenges. One thing is certain, the fact that emergencies happen.

- **In the occurrence of Simple Disasters**
  Even in a simple disaster, many lives could be lost or exposed to danger due to a lack of preparation. Many people may not have the requisite information or skills to rescue themselves and others. You do not want to be amongst that group of people with zero ability to make a difference in a life or death scenario.

- **When you are left with no options**
  What do you do when you are left with no options in the event of an emergency? What happens when the structure of modern society collapses and makes help difficult to access? What happens when everyone, including the government, is too busy saving themselves to save you?
  You may not have the luxury of time to wait for help and your country's support system. You may come to regret lacking simple survival skills, which could save your life in a crisis. It is better to be over-prepared than under-prepared!

- **Better Equipped!**
  In the occurrence of a disaster, you are better equipped to survive. When the anticipated disaster happens, you are confident of what to do. This would save you a lot of time and paranoia.
  As much as people believe their instincts may come to their rescue during a disaster, they may turn out to be unreliable. Why depend on your instincts in trying times when you can arm yourself with knowledge and experience within a controlled environment?

- **Survival is a basic human Instinct**
  Survival is a basic human instinct; humans and animals constantly strive to survive and adapt to their environment.

- **Speedy Recovery**
  In the occurrence of a catastrophe, only people who have prior plans would be less affected. After the emergency has come and gone, they would still be able to continue life without experiencing too much of its negative impacts.

The signs are encouraging. A survey conducted in 2020 found that approximately 141 million Americans, or half the US population, are preparing for emergencies with a focus on doomsday[1].

Doomsday is the school of thought that believes that some sort of disaster could wipe out a country or a large chunk of the world. While that may be the worst-case

---

[1] Richard Laycock, "Doomsday Preppers Statistics". Finder. Updated 19 Feb 2020. https://www.finder.com/doomsday-prepper-statistics

scenario, the important question to ask is, how do you start prepping if you have totally no experience?

Chapter 2: How to Start Prepping

Here are some questions to ponder about prepping.
- Are you preparing financially?
- Are you preparing for doomsday?
- Are you preparing for a military invasion?
- Do you want to protect your family?
- Are you preparing for other emergency scenarios?

There is so much money you can spend on prepping, but you'd need to direct your focus to what exactly you are preparing for, and what you can afford financially. Here you would appreciate the community setting of prepping; you could find different people preparing for things entirely different from yours, and they become a potential companion in the event of a disaster.

Irrespective of the different reasons for our preparation, there is a common ground denoted by the basic needs of every person. The needs include:

- **Food**
  Medical experts estimate the human ability to survive without food to be three weeks, at maximum. As preppers, food supply is indispensable to survival; depending on the nature of the emergency, you may be needing a lot of energy supply to thrive.

  A rule of thumb for preppers is that you are required to store food, but a little guidance would be required when it comes to storing food. You wouldn't want to store food you can't consume, cook, or would get spoilt in storage.

Preppers usually give priority to food items that do not require refrigeration and possess a longer shelf life. Generally, preppers store food to last for at least two weeks. Obviously, the quantity of food stored varies from individual to individual depending on the average calorie count.

Some preppers choose to grow certain types of food so they can be easily available during emergencies. It is also crucial to note that the food stored must be ready to eat or easy to cook by unconventional means. Preppers may consider the difficulties in accessing gas or electricity in a disruption. One popular class of food items among preppers is food bars, as they contain high energy compounds. They would come in handy during emergencies, without taking up too much space in your stockpile.

- **Water**
  If I were to order this list according to priority, water ranks higher than food. Medical experts estimate a maximum of three days to survive without water.
  By all means possible, you must find innovative means of storing pure water; one such means is a water filter. A water filter decontaminates and ensures a store of pure water is easily facilitated.

- **Air**

    Preppers try to avoid any shortage of air supply. Air ranks high above food and water because three minutes of its absence means certain death. Artificial store of air is the only way to prepare for emergencies that may affect air quality. Gas masks could be purchased to prepare for this scenario. While there are very few disasters that affect air supply, the goal of prepping is to prepare for the worst.

The three subjects discussed form the common ground all preppers share with regards to prepping. Having established this common connection, how do you start prepping?

1. **Ascertain Your Reason for Prepping**

    This is the first step when you want to start prepping. The preparation and financial cost involved in preparing against an apocalypse cannot be compared to a preparation to survive food and water scarcity. Take a pen and a journal, and note down why have you decided to start prepping.

2. **Take note of Common Needs**

    There is no prepping without the essentials for survival (food, water, shelter, security). You can store only water and food, but arrangements can be made for shelter and security.

3. **Create an Itemized List**
    Having defined your reason you would need to identify what you would need to prepare. If you are preparing against a possible food shortage, you would need your food journal to identify what items to stockpile according to calorie counts. If you are preparing to strengthen your defense you would need to list down some equipment, self-defense skills and other factors related to your preparation.

4. **Act Upon Your List of Preparations**
    Act out your preparations immediately. Do you need to stockpile more food, or purchase some survival kits? You should also start acquiring relevant skills and equipment.

5. **Make Plans for Evacuation and Emergency**
    Make plans for evacuation; most preppers have a bug out bag in case they need to evacuate urgently. These bags contain enough to supply and sustain them during the crisis. With regard to an emergency, you would need to have plans for reaching loved ones immediately and evacuating them from the area of crisis. Other emergency plans range from cash, identifications, relevant medical records to possible locations to get help.

6. **Prepping is Better Off as a Lifestyle**

Prepping does not stop once you are done procuring the items in your list. Prepping as a lifestyle is more beneficial, as there could be emergencies or factors that you did not account for initially. Try to join a prepping community or establish one of your own. This way, you are always prepared and able to call out for additional help. A good place to start is by getting family members, co-workers and friends interested in prepping, especially if you live alone.

Chapter 3: Basic Survival Skills

A lot has been said about prepping in the previous pages, and while discussing prepping, the word **"survival"** unavoidably appears. Prepping is preparation for some sort of catastrophic occurrence. Now, not many times are we sure of these unpalatable events happening, but we know that at some point, they may surface.

But why do we prepare? We prepare because we want to survive these extreme events with a reduced effect on our lives, as compared to a scenario where we had not prepared.

What is Survival?

The Oxford dictionary defines survival as the state or fact of continuing to live or exist, typically in spite of an accident, ordeal, or difficult circumstances.

Humans are made to be survivors; we are constantly adapting, learning, and adjusting as long as it means we would survive. As much as survival is inherent or instinctive, survival is at the mercy of certain information and skillsets. Prepping breaches the gap by providing the necessary skills, materials, and combination of information needed to ensure your survival against all odds.

Survival Skills

Survival skills are the skillsets a prepper must possess to ensure he/ she survives in the occurrence of a catastrophic event. As much as everyone is a "survivor," preppers have an advantage due to the training or arrangements made for various scenarios.

We shall soon discuss a number of skillsets recommended by veteran preppers which are essential for surviving a disaster.

However, before you rush into learning all these skills, it is important to first identify your strengths and weaknesses. Instead of focusing on learning new skills in your weak area, a more effective strategy may be to focus on your strengths, and find other preppers who are strong in your weak areas. This is where a community is useful.

These essential skillsets listed below are not arranged in any order of priority; nevertheless, they are required in many emergency situations.

- **Procuring Essentials**
  Simply put, you'd need any skill that facilitates ensuring your food, water, and shelter are guaranteed. With regards to shelter, you would need to be safe from the weather and every other thing that poses a threat. Depending on prevailing weather condition, you would find the skill of making a fireplace useful.

  Regarding water and food, you will need to either have pre-stocked supplies or obtain food and pure water from your environment safely. The shelter can be portable, but in a case where there's no shelter, learning to make a shelter from what is available in your environment would be your only option.

- **Making Fire**
  You need to know how to light a fire and keep it burning for as long as you want, especially when you have to stay outdoors for a period of time. There are a number of kits that could help you out with lighting a fire, but if you do not have the kits on hand, you would have to learn the primitive way of making fire. Fire is essential to keep you warm, purify water, cook meals, as well as keep you away from animals and other insects.

- **Navigation**
  Many emergencies are outdoor in nature or force us to stay outdoors, so there is a need to master the art of navigation. A compass and map are important for navigation. Ensure your compass is reputable and trustworthy before you begin your exploration.

  Also, you could consider putting small signs along hiking trails or terrain that is near you. They can serve as a vantage point. Besides learning how to use a map and compass to navigate, you could also consider learning the art of using the sun and stars to navigate.

- **Self-Defense**
  Security may not be the first thing on your mind. However, you may be surprised to find out that your neighbor or other human beings would pose a threat to your life in a crisis. This is due to your supplies- if you have prepped well, they could attract others who are desperate for food and water.

Learning how to use firearms and some basic martial arts would come in handy. If you run out of ammo, skills such as taekwondo, boxing, or Krav Maga would become necessary. Take note that while there are many online tutorial videos about martial arts, I do not recommend relying fully on those for training. While YouTube videos may give you a good sense of the type of martial art you may be drawn towards, if you are serious about it, you should find a certified trainer. This is to prepare you for the real-world scenario, where you might have to deal with competent opponents.

- **First Aid**
First aid is an essential skill for keeping yourself or your loved ones alive long enough before standard medical help becomes available. Within the area of first aid, skills ranging from cardio-pulmonary resuscitation (CPR) to dressing wounds to immobilizing broken bones are all very beneficial.

- **Communication and Sending a Signal**
Learning to communicate effectively in the event of compromised cell lines or shutdown of communication channels is paramount for survival. There are numerous alternate means of communication over varying distances. If you wish to send a distress signal over longer distances, you must be at the highest point in the locality so your signal can be seen. Distress signals could be made using flares, torch lights,

fires, radio beacons, fog horns and various communication devices.

NB: I strongly recommend that YouTube tutorial videos on each of these skills be sourced from reputable trainers. These could be a good starting point to learn about amazing survival tricks you do not know. However, learning in person from a qualified trainer is almost always better, as you would have a controlled environment to practice and correct errors.

Chapter 4: Survival Attitudes

What are Survival Attitudes?

I am of the opinion that survival is inherent in everyone; the same goes for survival attitudes. Attitude can be defined as the state of mind; the emphasis is on the word state, which means it varies with scenarios.

Survival attitude is simply a set of characteristics you must cultivate in the state of your mind to increase your chances of survival. You would access the wealth of information at your disposal through prepping.

By default, prepping should help your survival attitude. Nevertheless, if you suffer from issues such as clinical depression and mental disorders, it is important to see a professional physician or therapist regularly, and continue with all prescribed medications. It is also important that a close family member keeps track of your progress and also shares your interest in prepping and survival.

Survival attitudes include overcoming fear to achieve a positive outcome, and courage and optimism despite facing disaster. Only a few would have these attitudes well-cultivated naturally.

Conversely, many people survive because of the wealth of information obtained from prepping. When you attend classes to acquire skills, you would find out there are many things you could not do by instinct alone.

Being prepared would also help you gain confidence and put you in a positive frame of mind should disaster strike. Sometimes, all it takes is a small bit of information or a skill that you acquired previously to dramatically increase your chances of survival.

Chapter 5: A Prepper's Supply Checklist

A preppers checklist refers to a list of items you must have in your survival kit in the occurrence of an emergency. Now, I could go on about some 200 items you must have in supply, but for the sake of being brief, I will only discuss the most relevant and important.

- First on the list would be your food supply. You should have food stored at home, as well as a bug out bag with food supplies in case of evacuation.
- Water: Three days without water, and you are dead so, have sufficient water as well as a water filter.
- Portable shelter, more like a tent, or get some tools that would facilitate erecting a shelter.
- A portable energy source
- Flashlight or alternate source of light
- Fire-starters to light fire successfully
- Fuel for cooking/ powering your shelter
- Medical alcohol in your first aid kit
- Emergency medication including antihistamines, antacids, antibiotics, aspirin, and charcoal capsules in your first aid kit
- Toothbrushes, toothpaste, toilet paper, and other necessary hygiene-related supplies
- Shortwave radio, walkie-talkies, whistles and other communication devices, and spare batteries for these. One or a combination of these items is usually sufficient, depending on the nature of the emergency.
- Cash in hand
- Identification cards and medical records
- Firearms

- Kitchenware
- Any other item that you think is important in case of an emergency. Naturally, the type of emergency you are preparing for determines the supply checklist you would need to have.

These notions about preppers are wrong!

There are many common misconceptions about prepping and survival. Those who do not understand why you do this may hold some of these misconceptions. This is why many preppers do not like discussing prepping with non-preppers. Let's clear the air a little:

- **Preppers are Paranoid**
  If people believe that preppers are unnecessarily paranoid, this means half the American population is paranoid. Regardless, being prepared just means that you would be more confident in the uncertainty life may bring you. Instead of always worrying about unforeseen circumstances, preppers may actually become more stable and balanced. Prepping reduces the fear and panic a person has of the uncertainties brought about by a crisis.

- **Prepping is for the Rich**
  It is true that prepping would cost you a significant amount of cash, but it is equally false that prepping is for the rich. There are levels of prepping; the most basic prepping endeavors are generally affordable for the average person. The consolation to prepping is the fact that money doesn't deter us from investing in safety protocols for our family and loved ones.

- **Preppers Live in Isolation**
  Preppers do not leave in isolation; they could be your friends, siblings, co-worker and even neighbor next door. Many do not live in bunkers, woods, or secluded places; preppers live a "normal life" by most definitions.

- **Preppers are Irrational**
  A school of thought believes that preppers are irrational with their thoughts because they anticipate an apocalypse. I would like to reemphasize that preparing for an apocalypse is not all there is to prepping. An apocalypse may be the ultimate worst-case scenario that a prepper might think of after fulfilling all the lower levels of prepping. There are many other emergency scenarios that you have to account for, such as earthquakes, war, famine and a viral outbreak.

  At the end of the day, those who live the prepping lifestyle would be better equipped to handle a crisis, and should the unthinkable happen, they could be among the survivors.

In addition to misconceptions about preppers, there are many myths about survival. Here we would explore some of them:

- **72 Hours Would Do for an Emergency Plan**
  This myth has no factual backing; by experience, we know that most emergencies, disasters, or catastrophic experiences are not short-lived. They may extend for up to a week or more. Most times, preppers are advised to have an emergency plan for at least a two-week period.

- **You Can Depend on the Government in Times of Crisis**
  As much you wish you could count on the government for your security and safety, in the event of a disaster, you might have to depend on yourself. Catastrophic events usually result in millions of people seeking help from the government. In some cases, the government may not have been prepared for the crisis.

  Besides, the government system can never be perfect as long as people are in charge of the offices. Some government employees will also be affected by a crisis, and they may be faced with hard choices. So, let the government be your last or backup option when you have exhausted all other means of survival.

- **Being A Loner Equals Survival**
  This is another survival myth; in reality, being in a group gives you much better odds of surviving a crisis. A community may provide much-needed help and assistance in your areas of deficiency. You do not have the luxury of being an island of knowledge, and you may not have been prepared beyond the basic level.

  With a community of people, the stress that comes with emergencies is evenly distributed with more people. For instance, imagine having to protect yourself and sleep at the same time in the wild! In contrast, members of a group could take turns performing tasks so that no one becomes mentally and emotionally drained.

- **Misunderstanding of Natural Phenomena**
  In your bid to survive, you must be careful not to misunderstand some natural phenomena. For example, you may be wrong to assume that birds are always headed in the direction of the water. Trying to follow their trails or path may land you in bigger trouble. You need discretion and instincts to make some survival decisions. Remember to always plan and reevaluate. Sometimes survival is about trusting your instincts when you have not fully prepared for the scenario.

- **Forging Ahead Equals Survival**
  Forging ahead does not always guarantee survival. It depends on the nature of the crisis. You should get going only when there is a clear need to proceed from your location. The more you roam about, the more you would expose yourself to dangers. Preppers recommend that you stay put in a safe place, and only forge ahead when there is an obvious reason to.

- **Boiled Water is Safe to Drink**
  Boiled water does not always mean pure water. While much of the germs in water could be killed after boiling, it could have been contaminated by fuel or unknown chemicals in the first place. If you are unsure about the water's source, it may be safer to drink bottled water from your supplies. Nevertheless, boiling is still useful if you are obtaining water in the wild. If you are unable to boil water, you could use filters and disinfectants to purify it.

Survival Tips

Since this guide focuses on newbies, it would be wise to help you with a few additional survival tips. These tips range from specific scenarios to general information in case of emergency. Take note that these are not exhaustive:

- Never attempt to suck the spot of a snake bite as a form of remedy. It is medically unsafe and unhealthy; instead, use snake bite kits while waiting for medical help.
- If you are attacked by an animal while outdoors and you do not have weapons on hand, look for sensitive parts like the eyes of the animal to attack. For example, hurting a shark in its eyes increases the chances of it taking its grip off you.
- Never hide under an overpass during a tornado; you may have heard it is the right thing to do. But advanced studies show that you put yourself at more risk of disaster.
- If you see a bear, hold your ground. Do not attempt to run, they would outrun you any time of the day, and they can climb trees really well. Hold your ground, stretch out your arms so that you would appear bigger, and slowly and calmly disappear out of sight. If a black bear attacks you, try your best to escape to a secure area. If a brown bear attacks you, the best way to escape is by playing dead. Lay down on the ground with your pack on if possible, and protect your neck with your hands.

- Never take the risk of staying put in the occurrence of a hurricane. Regardless of the category rating, evacuate as soon as possible!
- Keep your hygiene standards high. You would need to be healthy to survive emergencies. Besides, a pandemic can easily be transmitted across countries. Stay healthy and fit!
- In the event of a respiratory crisis, note that bandanas only protect you from people and larger particles. They do not protect you from microorganisms.
- Alcohol does not warm you up but lowers your body temperature. Avoid taking alcohol as a source of warmth.

Preparing Before You Leave Home

The idea behind being a prepper is to always be prepared, so; we do not leave our homes without some basic supplies. An emergency could take place anywhere. It could happen while we are on our way to work, school or on a night out.

Preppers carry their Get Home bags; this is not very different from a Bug Out Bag. This bag can be placed in your car; it would be absurd to carry the bag with you everywhere you go. The bag contains most of the supplies in your bug out bag, but may differ in quantity. The supplies in the bag are intended to ensure your safety while away from home. You could also use your Get Home Bag to help a stranger who is facing an emergency.

While preparing for an emergency, it is important to note that your house must have supplies as well as survival kits that can serve for more than 72 hours. If the outbreak of any crisis requires you to stay indoors, your home must have sufficient supplies to sustain you and your family for two weeks.

For example, the outbreak of the pandemic coronavirus in 2020 necessitated that many people across the globe remained indoors. Those who do not have prior preparation in such situations may have issues with sustenance, given government restrictions on movement.

What Are Bug Out Bags?

Bug out bags are your emergency getaway pack. They contain supplies to last you more than seventy-two hours when a crisis hits. Below is the checklist of a typical Bug Out Bag.

- 32 oz potable water stored in a hard canteen
- Fire kit with tinder
- Lighter x 2
- Multitool
- Water filter
- Collapsible canteen/ vessel
- Cordage x 50.'
- Water purification tablets x 20-40
- Headlamp
- Socks
- Ready-to-eat food
- Toilet paper
- Field knife
- Nail clippers
- Respirator
- Documents (physical and USB thumb drive)

- Cash
- Tarp
- Waterproof paper and pen
- Pants
- Storage bags (20L dry bag and 5x gallon Ziplock bags)
- Condensed soap
- One- or two-way radio
- Jacket / outer shell
- USB charging cable and wall plug
- Top base layer
- Shemagh / bandana / gaiter
- Contractor trash bags x 2
- Li-Ion battery pack
- Hat
- Underwear

NB: Contents of your bug out bag can vary depending on the emergency you are preparing for and the size of your bug out bag.

Conclusion

After understanding the basics of prepping and survival, it is clear that everyone should be involved in prepping endeavors. First, prepping isn't all about some doomsday apocalypse; it goes beyond that. It is preparing for any form of emergency, and emergencies would surely occur in life.

Prepping doesn't have to be expensive; neither is it only for the rich. An average person can be a prepper without having to strain themselves financially.

Prepping always starts from a basic level, but once you are confident, you may choose to progress to a higher level of preparation. Ultimately, the best decision you can make in times of relative comfort is to become a prepper. This is because when disaster strikes, you may not have time to react if you do not practice the prepping lifestyle in the first place.

Was This Book Beneficial to You?

Thank you for picking up this book. It is my hope that you would take up prepping and learn more about surviving in various emergency situations.

If you think this information is useful, I would appreciate if you could share it with friends and family members. This is the book's official listing page: https://www.amazon.com/dp/B086R1YJDY/

I would also like to read your reviews about this book. They are really important to me, as they will help me to

improve in future works. You may leave a review at this page:
http://www.amazon.com/review/create-review?&asin=B086R1YJDY

About the Author

Ever since stumbling upon the prepping and survival interest eight years ago, Ernest has been studying different facets of preparing for emergencies. Besides stocking up on supplies and equipment, he also loves watching documentaries on how animals survive in the wild.